You Fit the Bill for a Perfect Friend

AF580921

ILLUSTRATED BY

Suzy Spafford

Suzy's Zoo

HARVEST HOUSE PUBLISHERS

EUGENE, OREGON

You Fit the Bill for a Perfect Friend

Text Copyright © 2004 by Harvest House Publishers
Eugene, Oregon 97402

ISBN 0-7369-1418-8

Original artwork © Suzy Spafford. Suzy's Zoo® is a registered trademark of Suzy's Zoo, A California Corporation.

Design and production by Garborg Design Works, Minneapolis, Minnesota

Harvest House Publishers has made every effort to trace the ownership of all poems and quotes. In the event of a question arising from the use of a poem or quote, we regret any error made and will be pleased to make the necessary correction in future editions of this book.

Unless otherwise indicated, all Scripture quotations are taken from the HOLY BIBLE, NEW INTERNATIONAL VERSION®. NIV®. Copyright©1973, 1978, 1984 by the International Bible Society. Used by permission of Zondervan. All rights reserved.

All rights reserved. No part of this publication may be reproduced, stored in a retrieval system, or transmitted in any form or by any means—electronic, mechanical, digital, photocopy, recording, or any other—except for brief quotations in printed reviews, without the prior permission of the publisher.

Printed in China

04 05 06 07 08 09 10 11 12 13 / LP / 10 9 8 7 6 5 4 3 2 1

To:

From:

You fit the bill for a perfect friend!

You follow the golden rule of friendship: Birds of a feather flock together.

So long as we are loved by
others I should say
That we are almost indispensable;
And no man is useless while
he has a friend.

ROBERT LOUIS STEVENSON

I knew the minute you called me "friend" that I would never feel alone or on the outside again.

What is a friend? A single

Friendship without self-
interest is one of the rare
and beautiful things in life.
JAMES FRANCIS BYRNES
soul dwelling in two bodies.
ARISTOTLE

You care for those you love.

There are persons so
radiant, so genial, so kind,
so pleasure-bearing,
that you instinctively feel
in their presence that they
do you good,
whose coming into a room
is like the bringing of
a lamp there.

HENRY WARD BEECHER

Shelter, kindness, love, affection—you shower such goodness on everyone in your life.

Happy is the house

Greater love has no one than this, that he lay down his life for his friends.

THE BOOK OF JOHN

"Friendship," said Christopher Robin, "is a very comforting sort of thing to have."

A.A. MILNE

that shelters a friend.

Ralph Waldo Emerson

I can count on you to be a true friend; after all, "if it walks like a duck..."

Whenever you are true to yourself, you will also be true to others.

ALEXANDRA STODDARD

When your circumstances change,
you remain the same. In you,
I have found a consistent, faithful friend.

True happiness consists not in the multitud

God be in my head,
And in my understanding;
God be in my eyes,
And in my looking;
God be in my mouth,
And in my speaking;
God be in my heart.

ANONYMOUS

Friendship is the hardest thing in the world to explain. It's not something you learn in school. But if you haven't learned the meaning of friendship, you really haven't learned anything.

MUHAMMAD ALI

of friends, but in their worth and choice.

SAMUEL JOHNSON

LOVE

When I am going in circles, you get my ducks in a row.

We are here to help each other, to try to make each other happy.

SAYING OF THE POLAR ESKIMOS

Somehow you know just what to do. You are my personal organizer, planner, and visionary.

A real friend is one who walks in when the rest of the world walks out.

WALTER WINCHELL

What I expect from my male friends is that they are polite and clean. What I expect from my female friends is unconditional love, the ability to finish my sentences for me when I am sobbing, a complete and total willingness to pour their hearts out to me, and the ability to tell me why the meat thermometer isn't supposed to touch the bone.

ANNA QUINDLEN

SEEDS
Pansy
SEEDS
Radish
SEEDS
Margo's
Basil
Parsley
Rose-mary
Sweet Pea
Great Northern Bean
Margo's Secret Grow Juice
Margo's Garden Center

Go Girl!

You think laughing out loud is not only acceptable, it is admirable!

Laughter is the closest thing to the grace of God.

KARL BARTH

I look to you for comic relief, for permission to laugh, and for an excuse to be silly.

We are all here for a spell;
Get all the good laughs you can.

WILL ROGERS

Savor the moments that are warm and special and giggly.

SAMMY DAVIS, JR.

Laughter is the shortest distance between two people.

VICTOR BORGE

When I lose my way, you bring me back to shore.

A friend hears the song
in my heart and sings it to me
when my memory fails.

ANONYMOUS

I can trust your guidance, advice, and gentle leading. Sometimes all I need is a nudge from you and the way back home is clear. And nothing looks finer.

Friends broaden our horizons. They serve as new models with whom we can identify. They allow us to be ourselves and accept us that way.

Judith Viorst

One of the surest evidences of friendship that one individual can display to another is telling him gently of a fault. If any other can excel it, it is listening to such a disclosure with gratitude, and amending the error.

EDWARD BULWER-LYTTON

The friend of my adversity I shall always cherish most. I can better trust those who helped to relieve the gloom of my dark hours than those who are so ready to enjoy with me the sunshine of my prosperity.

ULYSSES S. GRANT

You treat people with unconditional kindness.

Who is the happiest of men? He who values the merits of others, and in their pleasure takes joy, even as though it were his own.

GOETHE

When your heart gives, there are no strings attached. I receive your kindness freely, because I never have to search for hidden expectations or conditions.

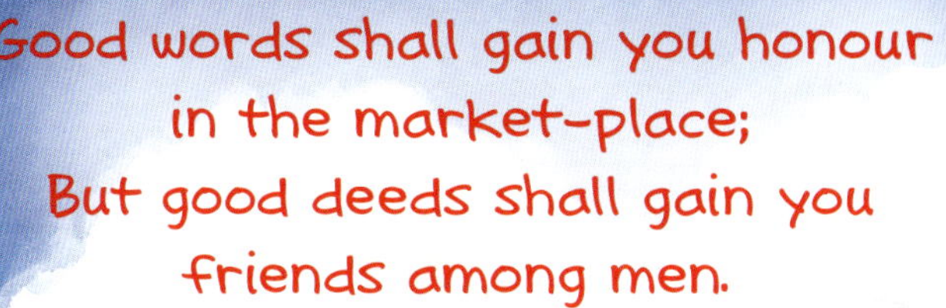
Good words shall gain you honour
in the market-place;
But good deeds shall gain you
friends among men.

LAO-TSE

When I think of my closest friendship—those in which I've grown, learned to compromise and negotiate, established boundaries—I notice that in every case they were built on a mutual ability to let each other be free.

LUCI SWINDOLL

Nothing ruffles your feathers.

We have been friends together
in sunshine and in shade.

CAROLINE NORTON

You are patient and forgiving.
I am lifted by your hopefulness.

When people are true friends,
even shared water tastes sweet.

CHINESE PROVERB

Hope is the thing with feathers
That perches in the soul,
And sings the tune without the words,
And never stops at all,

And sweetest in the gale is heard;
And sore must be the storm
That could abash the little bird
That kept so many warm.

EMILY DICKINSON

Friendship that flows from the heart cannot be frozen by adversity, as the water that flows from the spring cannot congeal in winter.

JAMES FENIMORE COOPER

Your smile makes my day.

There is not beautifier
of complexion, or form,
or behavior,
like the wish to scatter joy
and not pain around us.

VIRGIL

How do you do it? When I am having a really bad day, you just happen to stop by and make everything okay with a smile and a joke or two.

A faithful friend is

AUTHOR UNKNOWN

The rain may be falling hard outside,
But your smile makes it all alright.
I'm so glad that you're my friend.
I know our friendship will never end.

ROBERT ALAN

But friendship is precious, not only in the shade, but in the sunshine of life; and thanks to a benevolent arrangement of things, the greater part of life is sunshine.

THOMAS JEFFERSON

You make a splash wherever you go.

The ornament of a house is
The friends who frequent it.

RALPH WALDO EMERSON

I love how you can fill a room with your personality, yet you turn the spotlight on everyone else.

True friends have no solitary joy or sorrow.

CHANNING

Though friendship is not quick to burn, it is explosive stuff.

MAY SARTON

Each friend represents a world possibly not

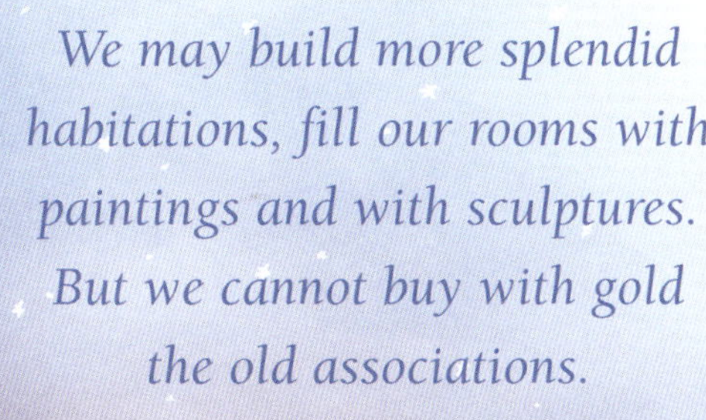

We may build more splendid habitations, fill our rooms with paintings and with sculptures. But we cannot buy with gold the old associations.

HENRY WADSWORTH LONGFELLOW

a world in us,
born until they arrive.

ANAÏS NIN

You chose me to be your friend.

However rare true love may be, it is less so than true friendship.

LA ROCHEFOUCAULD

I am blessed by our friendship. Thank you for choosing me to be a part of your life.

SUNFLOWER

I have loved my friend as I do virtue, my soul, my God.

SIR THOMAS BROWNE

I no doubt deserved
my enemies,
But I don't believe I
deserved my friends.

WALT WHITMAN

I'd like to be the sort of friend
That you have been to me;
I'd like to be the help
That you've been always glad to be;
I'd like to mean as much to you
Each minute of the day
As you have meant, old friend of mine,
To me along the way.

EDGAR A. GUEST

Friends are the sunshine of life.
John Hay